# KEEP SMILING

## ABUNDANCE HAPPENS!



ENTREPRENEUR 1.0
COLOR EDITION

ROBERT C. PETERSON
KEN 'DR. SMILEY' ROCHON, JR., PhD

Keep Smiling: Abundance Happens!



Entrepreneur 1.0
Color Edition

ISBN: 978-1-64810-185-4

Printed in the United States of America

# ACKNOWLEDGEMENTS & DEDICATIONS

The biggest joy I receive in the world is seeing my son Kenny (K3) smile. I have seen the power of his smile, and this book is my way of honoring him as well as a gentleman named Barry Shore for handing me a 'KEEP SMILING' card.

Thank you to Andrew Cordle, Michelle Mras, Noelle Peterson, Robert Peterson, Sally Wurr, Michael Schoening, and Todd Westra.

Thank you to Al Granger, Carolyn Sheltraw, and Dr. Andrea Adams-Miller.

Shift happens when you count your blessings, such as the people in your life who believe in you. No matter what happens in the world, you have the power to shift and when you do, you become more powerful.

*Dr. Smiley*

# PREFACE

An influencer is one of the most important and powerful responsibilities a person can have in this day and age. We, as a society, listen to influencers to make decisions on what we buy, what we like, what we love, and for what we vote. The people in this book have proven they use their influence for good.

This book is filled with over 100 influencers who generate positivity through their lifestyle choices, their messaging, and mostly through the sheer number of smiles they inspire.

Influencers who amplify goodness should be honored so they can influence even more smiles. Therefore, we created a book that helps you learn who you may want to follow and from who you may want to learn.

In a world in need of more smiles, we are so proud to honor the influencers in this book in hopes of making the world a more positive, powerful and happy place.

"Too often we underestimate the power of a touch, a smile, a kind word, a listening ear, an honest compliment, or the smallest act of caring, all of which have the potential to turn a life around."

~Leo Buscaglia

# THE AMBASSADOR OF JOY RESPONSIBLE FOR HANDING A CARD TO DR. SMILEY THAT STARTED IT ALL. :).

Barry Shore, The Ambassador of Joy with Dr. Smiley :)

# THE EVOLUTION OF DR. SMILEY

## BY

## KEN 'DR. SMILEY' ROCHON, JR., PhD

$36,000… that is what it would be worth to reach 10 million people. Do you want to reach 10 million people with your message? I do!

Most authors in a compilation book are never noticed or read. Why? Because there are too many chapters, and typically when you read one chapter, you may feel you have no reason or time to read more. This is connected to the value you received from the first chapter you selected.

If you select my chapter, this may be fortunate for you… as I intend to offer you $36,000 in value with no strings attached. Why? Because an author on a purpose driven life is not motivated by anything more than impact. So, if my chapter allows us to connect and share your story, then it will be a triumph and a compelling reason for writing this chapter.

When I was born over fifty years ago, I had no idea who 'Dr. Smiley' was, nor did I have any inclination he would be me.

I was born in Warwick, Rhode Island, and whisked away to Paris, France, as an Army brat. Twelve years and twelve countries later, I was back in Rhode Island trying to figure out how to use a phone. After devoting my life to soccer and believing this would be my life, I was depressed and disappointed that the return to America would be void of my biggest passion… Soccer. Pele was my role model, and he could not prepare me for the life I would lead in a small farm town in Galesburg, Illinois. This town was so isolated, that I was accused of being a 'Nazi Nigger Lover' because I came from Germany and was unaware that discrimination was a way of life in this town. The school was integrated, but the real estate told a different story. If you were on this side of the tracks, you were white, and the other side was predominantly black.

The reason I share this part of my life was that my dad and mom never taught me about discrimination or that it even existed. My mom was a fan of the American Indian and made it clear that the 'White Man' was the culprit of fairness and freedom. Her last thoughts as a victim of Alzheimer's were to support the American Indian and expose the atrocities of the White Man on this beautiful culture and race. Mind you, my mom is white, married to a white man.

I always wanted to be an author and more importantly matter in the world. I defined being an author as someone who was credible and worthy of attention and merit. Over thirty years of believing this never caused me to even write one sentence in a book… until I was a caregiver for my mom. That was the catalyst to stepping into my power---one born of fear I would die before I ever did anything to make a difference. I am not sure if all humans feel this way, but I certainly knew I could not be a person without a book.

This ignited action and a book thirteen months after my mom passed… titled 'Becoming the Perfect Networker… Succeeding 1 Connection @ a Time'.

This was a financial disaster, and any sane person would have written off the $22,000 loss as an act of ignorance. But a prayer to God helped me understand this was a message that most authors experience---perhaps a smaller financial loss, perhaps larger. Most quit with this impossible challenge to get a return on the investment (save the return on the effort). I would have quit, too, but God was clear… this was a lesson on how messed up self-publishing could be for a new author.

God and my mom were teaching me my most valuable lesson… a Legacy is earned with an unstoppable attitude. I invested another $3000 to republish and reprint this grammatically incorrect nightmare. It was grammatically incorrect because of hiring a college professor in Florida that obviously did not have a clue about editing or writing. He fleeced me for over $1000, and a lesson was learned that without social proof, testimonials, and vetting, you are positioning yourself as a lamb ready to be fleeced or slaughtered of any dreams you will chase in the future.

Perfect Publishing was born because of this nightmare. My valuable lesson created a much needed company to protect future authors of bad decisions. I learned quickly how many leaders would love to do their book but just didn't understand how to complete it. I learned this firsthand by offering a $5000 'How to Write Your Book' program for FREE. Roughly ten people joined this program, and only one completed it. Why? Because it is confusing and overwhelming. How could I help more people step into their power to be an author, an inspiration, and a legacy for the people they loved? I needed to go back to the drawing board and find out where the pitfalls are that stop people.

The first pitfall was being inspired enough to even do the book / project. Many leaders just didn't know if they were worthy of being Authors. Many thought 'I need to accomplish more before I can write this book', or 'I need more money, success, or perfection in my life'. Not knowing the gifts they had to share with the world already existed in their hearts and minds.

My focus became on how to overcome this challenge. I figured it out with some very simple out of the box techniques that caused almost 100% of my writers to become authors. It was about inspiration and breaking down the project into bite size weekly portions. Typically, a leader was able to complete this process in 3 to 6 months when I finally understood the dynamics of what would motivate them to compete, complete, and lunge into the finish line of being the new identity of an author.

The second issue became very clear to me that moving a book required a marketing approach and system---one fueled by social proof and testimonials. This was another gap that was causing authors great frustration. Most authors (almost 99%) were writing their first book, and the sales were so low that there just wasn't a desire to write another book. "Why would I write another book after I just wrote my best book… that took my life to create?" This was the question that was either internally plaguing them or that was shared with me with despair and disgust.

It was evident that there must be an approach or sequence that is causing this demise of the author's impact. It was quickly cleared up when I looked up their Amazon book listing and their social media. It was as if they believed that the book being delivered from their hearts and minds would magically awaken the world or through some osmosis would get into their avatars' being. I later termed this the Doctor Delivering the Baby (book) methodology. Basically, that when the book is printed, magically the world will find out about this birth.

As I have studied this insane perspective that the world is awaiting your book (unless you are an influencer with an enormous following), there is no one who knows your book exists… save the family you shared this dream with and your friends that will out of obligation buy your book for $20 with almost no intention of consuming, sharing, or being impacted by your brilliance. Because your friends know you, they have a difficult time adjusting to see you be bigger than how they define you in their lives.

This challenge is universal. Hence the reason when you make it big, your friends show up sharing they know you. ☺ Unless your friends have influence, I have learned it is best to show up as an unknown and create an identity you wish to be taken serious for being. I recently became 'Dr. Smiley'. This was welcomed in the new world. But it just could not be taken seriously by my family… well, my son loves the name and probably overstates my fame at this point. But having a young son to motivate you to be his hero is a gift in and of itself.

What I have learned is that I was almost 99% incorrect in how much proportion of my resources (money and time) should be spent on making my book versus moving my book. It turns out that if you spend three months or even one year writing your book, you are only doing what an Olympic athlete would do to get to the starting line of his/her performance or race. In other words, if you only wrote a book and thought that all the writing was the win, you would be thinking that all your workouts to qualify to be in the Olympics should be a medal earned. You have earned almost nothing by printing your book. I don't say this to be cruel or dissuade you from a wonderful accomplishment for your immediate family and friends. I am only putting this in perspective that there are over 7 billion people on this planet. What percentage are you impacting, inspiring, and causing to be fans of your passion and purpose?

My goal when I complete a book is never to stop marketing or printing it. That changes the book accomplishment to almost 1% of the work. I spend about 99% of my resources (money and time) making sure the book has impact. The closer I am able to be to 99%, the closer I have found the book impacts the world instead of only qualifying to compete to qualify to be at the Olympics. ☺

My final awakening of publishing is the misconception of moving a book versus creating abundance. A book is not just a delivery project to your family or even the world; it is hopefully a means of positioning you to be a solution, a leader, an expert, a sought-after sage of your domain. My book 'Becoming the Perfect Networker... Succeeding 1 Connection @ a Time' positioned me as 'The Man Who Wrote the Book on Networking'. I was on over 50 podcasts, and I became relevant to people who were just going to networking events and collecting cards. I became a prodigy of Bob Burg's 'Go-Giver' which inspired me to stop networking and start 'net-giving'. Instead of focusing on me, I moved to focus on who I could connect my network to create synergy, collaborations, joint ventures, and ultimately fans of my KEEP SMILING movement. The book broke several unofficial world records. It was the first book to have a ribbon on the front cover stating, 'Almost 100 Books Sold'. This little red ribbon was one of the biggest reasons I was selected to be on so many podcasts. They shared you are either very funny or crazy. Either way, it will make for a great show.

This book was also the first book to start on page '-1' and proceed to page '0' featuring the chapter 'The Defeatist Attitude' in order to make the point we must shift from believing we are not powerful to believing we create our happiness, our life, and our success. There were several other aspects that made this book a groundbreaking success in bringing business---humor (and color illustrations) together to provide the reader with page turning engagement and smiles.

My interests turned to publishing and writing books that didn't seem to exist on searches I did for children's books, linguistics, travel, etc. An eight-year dive into a project titled 'Making Friends Around the World' would be the first 'Decalingual' book in history.

In 2015, I met a man whom I lovingly refer to as a 'Prophet of Joy'. His name is Barry Shore. He simply handed me a card with 'KEEP SMILING' as the two words that would awaken my soul much like John Belushi in the movie 'The Blues Brothers' where he 'Sees the Light' and does cartwheels after experiencing James Brown and a concretion literally flipping and flying in the air with jubilation. I couldn't stop thinking about how congruent this message was to my mom's ability to bring positivity to my life, my family, her students, and her friends.

I shared with Barry that this card had awakened my soul, and I believe after his responses to what he is doing with the card, that I could create a movement. Little did he know that day that the card would be photographed thousands of times with amazing authors, business entrepreneurs, leaders, models, musicians, speakers, and anyone sporting a beautiful smile (teeth or not).

With all these photos taken, it was an easy decision to see what would happen if I created and published a little 6 x 6 book with all these amazing smiles and choose one of the leaders to share their story. We have almost 200 of these thematic books on Amazon and on our website (www.theKEEPSMILINGmovement.com) for FREE. Special thanks to our executive director, Dr. Andrea Adams, for her tireless commitment to keeping the movement … moving. She put on the map a legitimate 501c nonprofit with a mission of helping save lives with dental and mental wellness. The book 'The Science of Smiles' was released to share the importance of Smiles as part of your daily nutrition for your soul.

After completing my 36th book 'The Amazon 5 Star Review Club' book, I feel I have unleashed possibly my best work. It is a free book I provide to help authors get access to amazing content and return their appreciation in the form of a review on Amazon. This is the ultimate thank you to authors who have basically shared their souls for the sole purpose of impacting your life.

I've found my best strategy for making a difference in the world… is keep writing and keep giving my books away to people who need a solution to something I have written about. I average giving over 1 thousand books away a year (pre-pandemic) and over 10 thousand books a year as eBooks. If your book inspires someone to be better or awakens them to focus on you as a solution to their happiness, I assure you life will be better for both of you.

My favorite year of my life is ironically 2020---not because of the pandemic, of course, but because of what the pandemic caused, created, and inspired… a renaissance in my life and my son. Before the pandemic, my son (Kenny Rochon, III, aka K3) was not an author. He now has 6 books and aims on having 10 by his tenth birthday. His first book was simply a joke book that was in essence a compilation of jokes we found on Google that made him laugh. This book put him on the map because of the strategy I created around his book. He currently has over 150 five-star reviews for all his books because he understands at age 8 how to convert sales into testimonials and reinvest his profits proportionally into future books.

It was also the year I started my dissertation through the International University of Entrepreunology with a PhD in Philosophy. This gave rise to a new way of being identified… 'Dr. Smiley'. I come from a family of high learners, so this was a prestigious advance on my degrees, but my true motivations were to make my mom proud, and for my son to see when the chips are down, you can still come out on top if you want this enough.

My biggest legacy triumph is and probably will be my son's renaissance into authorship during this year of uncertainty. To my son, the pandemic was an opportunity to be home and not have to go to school. He didn't know what hit him when I shared I would be teaching him what he was missing… if he was in college. He questioned me several times asking me if I was sure a second grader should know the military alphabet, countries, and flags of the world, the periodic table, and sign language. I responded, 'Only if you are going to be a future leader'. He bought it, and we worked on his grasp of knowing the above with competency that would impress any adult. We soon discussed the possibility of him being an author before his 7th birthday. He was open to this as it was a book entitled 'Kenny's Favorite Jokes'. He even had a page with some of his originals which will remain my favorite forever.

When the book was delivered to him on his birthday (June 14th / 'Flag Day'), he was concerned with only one thing… is it on Amazon and could I prove it. The delivery of this beautiful color book created only about 1% of the excitement he expressed when he did indeed see his book and name on Amazon.com. This was one of my proudest moments as a father.

He has since arranged, googled, searched, and put together 'Kenny's Favorite Riddles', 'Kenny's Favorite Science Facts', 'Kenny's Favorite Things to Know' and 'Kenny's Favorite Trivia'. He is finally paying tribute to his birthday theme of patriotism with his newest book 'Kenny's Favorite Places in America' with shoutouts to his favorite restaurant 'Mission BBQ' that he hopes will show off his books at all 150 restaurants.

Future projects are 'Kenny's Favorite Phobias to Conquer' which will help children and maybe even adults overcome fears that are only in their head.

The reason I chose to invest in being a contributor of this wonderful book is because I believe in a publisher bringing together amazing leaders and creating a collaboration of heart centered thought leaders who together bring more focus to this project because they work together to share it matters.

To return to my opening sentence… '$36,000… that is what it would be worth to reach 10 million people. Do you want to reach 10 million people with your message?' I do. This is my mark and largest project of my life thus far. I intend to honor great inspiring leaders with a 'Chicken Soup meets TED Talk' formula for inspiring HOPE in the world. The project is titled 'D.O.S.E. of HOPE' and the acronym stands for the amazing chemicals God has created that are released when we feel alive and have 'HOPE' (Dopamine, Oxytocin, Serotonin, and Endorphins).

Just as Simon Sinek identified the importance of a company knowing the 'Why' and how to create a culture that attracts consumers who relate and become ambassadors of your brand, I decided to research the impact of asking the question 'Who Am I?' and 'How did I create my Who?'. Turns out the more we commit, devote, and invest (as referenced in Malcolm Gladwell's book 'Outliers'), the more we will create a 'Who' we love. This relationship to our love of ourselves allows us to create an equally powerful 'Why' otherwise known as a 'Purpose'. The higher the variable of 'Purpose' we claim as it relates to the needs of humanity, the higher our 'How' will be (also known as your 'Impact' in the world).

So the variables can be shown as:

Y x W x H = Sph
('Y' = You; 'W' = Why / Purpose; 'H' = How / Impact and 'Sph' = Smiles per Hour)

This is a TED talk in the making that I believe will even impress Simon Sinek. But I am most hopeful that it becomes a new way of looking how to shift our focus from things that will never make us happy to our happiness being derived from our ability to bring happiness to others and the world. The close second ingredient I work tirelessly to teach my son is the gratitude reflection time needed for us to have the capacity to understand that our power to impact the world is fueled by our gratitude for being alive.

A friend recently gave me a wonderful acronym for H.O.P.E. … 'Hold On Pain Ends'. This inspired a book to honor my mentor Barry Shore, aka 'The Ambassador of Joy' and my co-founder of the KEEP SMILING movement to publish our first book together… 'A Pocket Full of Acronyms'.

A venture called 'Amplifluence.com' is being launched as a tour around the world to help leaders have more impact with their message and mission in life. Michelle Mras, founder of the 'Hold My Crown' series, and Todd Westra are co-founders of something I believe will harness all the energy put into the KEEP SMILING movement and PerfectPublishing and create an impressive marketing system that helps authors be better speakers and speakers become (better) authors using funnels, monetization strategies designed to fuel their careers and dreams.

Every book I have mentioned in this chapter and the other 33 or so are all available for FREE because I believe a book is a business card with a big message designed to create conversations, opportunities, and legacy. Simply Kennect with me, and any and all of the ebooks are available for the asking.

My mom had an expression 'Look for the Good in People and You Will Always Find It'. I thank my mom every day I am alive to know that the world has good people worth amplifying their goodness… which is on over 2 million 'KEEP SMILING' cards that have been distributed to people who give the biggest gift that shows their soul at the highest frequency… a SMILE ☺

"A smile covers a
multitude of mistakes."

– Robert C. Peterson

Robert C. Peterson, Mindset Coach; Speaker; Author; Podcaster

**Robert G Allen**

"Unfrowns are Smiles that have not been inverted."

**AJ Aluthwala**

"Every time you smile at someone, it is an action of love, a gift to that person, a beautiful thing."

**Jesse Anastase**

"Smiling makes a fashion statement."

**Robert Angel**

"A smile is happiness you'll find right under your nose." –Tom Wilson

**Chuck Bader**

"Because of your smile, you make life more beautiful." – Thich Nhat Hanh

**Mark Barsocchini, Centennial State Santa**

"A smile can hide so many feelings, fear, sadness, heartbreak, but it also shows one other thing, strength."

**Phyllis Marlene Benstein**

"A smile captured in a photo will spread happiness forever."

**Greg Bond**

"Nothing is more beautiful than a smile
that has struggled through tears." –Demi Lovato

**Bob Burg, Author, Speaker**

"Smile and you will Wow them all the time."

**Jack Canfield, Author, *Chicken Soup for the Soul* Series**

"A smile unites the world much like a song with a contagious beat causes the world to dance."

**Grant Cardone**

"Keep smiling… and one day life will get tired of upsetting you."

**Floyd Carns**

"A smile is a curve that sets everything straight."

**Aaron Chambers**

"A warm smile is the universal language of kindness."
~ William Arthur Ward

**Travis Chappel, Podcaster**

"A smile shows the reflection of your mindset and spirit."

**Deborah Benefield**

"Keep smiling, you're beautiful."

**Kirk Chugg**

"If you smile when you are alone,
then you really mean it." – Andy Rooney

**Dr. Robert Cialdini, Founder & CEO, Influence at Work**

Robert Cialdini, a prolific business copywriter and fantastic marketer, he has amassed millions of followers for his advice in marketing and publicity due to the book *Influence: The Psychology of Persuasion.*

"When a smile is given to you, be grateful
and return it as often as possible."

**Jessica Conti**

"Keep smiling and be fearless!"

**Madeline Costa**

"Every smile has a silver lining"

**Quinn Cottle**

"Mission: Smile America!"

**Ben Dahlby**

"Smiling is the Best Idea!"

**Kevin Dugan**

"The greatest gift is a smile at the right time."

**Anthony Duncan**

"Your smile is a choice, make it often."

**Candace Duncan**

"Do something special for someone today: just give them a smile and you will be amazed at how much of a difference it makes."

**Jeremiah Evans**

"Smiles Influence the world and create a positive frequency."

**Bill Fairham**

"Smile and the world smiles with you."
–Stanley Gordon West

**Evva Fenison**

"A smile is the shortest distance between two people."

**April Anne Fink**

"Strong people know how to keep their life in order. Even with tears in their eyes, they still manage to say "I'm okay" with a smile."

**Dan Fleyshman**

"I hope you always find a reason to smile."

**April Joy Ford**

"A smile informs the world you are a person that welcomes happiness and also delivers it."

**Michael Grebas**

"Making someone smile can change the world. Maybe not the whole world, but their own world."

**Sandy Hancock**

"A smile is one of the best forms of flattery."

**Mark Victor Hansen, American inspirational and motivational speaker, trainer and author**

"There is fear when frowning. There is love when smiling." —Maxime Lagacé

**Kevin Harrington**

"The best thing you can produce in the world is a smile that inspires others."

**Ashley Hepburn**

"A smile a day keeps the opportunities in play."

**Scott Hillman**

"A planned smile is a well planned day."

**Wendy Ida**

"The most gorgeous feature on a woman is a knock out smile."

**Jayne**

"The more you smile, the more mojo you exude."

**Scott Jensen**

"When music touches the heart,
a smile soon follows."

**Daymond John**

"The best smile is the best value to your face."

**Chris Johnsen**

"Smile everyday and live longer."

**Rob Johnson, CEO Bachi Bus, DJ Heart Attack**

"Smiles create a future of smiles."

**Johnny Joy**

"4 every 1 smile you give, is a smile that is given to so many beyond that moment."

**Kimber Kalata**

"Make smiling a habit!"

**Aristotle Karas**

"Leaders measure their impact in smiles."

**Dr. Richard Kaye**

"You smiled at the stars like they knew all your secrets."

**Frank Kern**

"When we smile, we conquer doubt, fear, sadness and worry."

**Brandon James Kirk**

"Keep calm and keep smiling!"

**Flo Lattery**

"A smile is the prettiest thing
you'll ever wear."

**"G" Gaydon Leavitt**

"The absolute best gift you can give someone is a smile, it is like music to the soul."

**Chuck 'ICEMAN' Liddell**

"Smile captured is a memory for life."

**Lindsey Litton**

"Peace begins with a smile." — Mother Teresa

**Adri Loughmiller**

"Smile and be kind, for we are here in this world just for a while."

**Tom Luane**

"A smile is your authentic brand."

**Marshall**

"A smile is the universal welcome."
– Max Eastman

**Heather McBroom**

"The world always looks brighter from behind a smile."

**Andy McFarland**

"A smile is the light in your window that tells others that there is a caring, sharing person inside." ~ Denis Waitley

**Dallas McGee**

"Take a smile challenge often and see how many smiles you can create in an hour."

**Ellie Mcgee**

"Wellness happens when we think and grow smiles."

**Brad Mortensen**

"Swing that frown pendulum to a smile."

**Michelle Mras**

"When life gives you limes,
rearrange the letters until they say smile."

**Rafael Norwood**

"Illuminate your smile."

**Adam Oliver**

"A smile is a metaphysical phenomenon that shifts humanity every time it is experienced."

**John Pennington**

"Smiles can help you Survive every Cancer."

**Rey Perez**

"Beautiful Smile... Beautiful Life."

**Steve Pesavento**

"Stay strong. Make them wonder how you're still smiling."

**CJ Peterson**

"Smile and the universe smiles back."

**Noelle Peterson**

"Speakers smile and their message is heard better."

**Joan Pounds**

"You never get a chance to make a first impression... Just smile!"

**Jake Randall**

"Your attitude reflects the smile you wear every minute of the day."

**Carmelia Ray**

"The game of life is won the second you choose to make your smile your go to expression."

**Greg S. Reid, Author**

"Raise a child with smiles and
it will follow them through life."

**Tina Renee**

"Smiles influence abundance."

**Edward Rodgers**

"We shall never know all the good that a simple smile can do. "– Mother Teresa

**Nick Santonastasso**

"Smile to Infinity and beyond!"

**Samantha Sargent**

"The best way to start your day is with a smile. That is also the best way to end it. :)"

**Karyn Savory**

"A Smile is the best way to hypnotize the world to respond with happiness."

**Erin Saxton, C.E.O. at Eleven Communications & Speaker**

"Sometimes all it takes is a smile to make everything feel better."

**Marya Schoening**

"Have a colorful smile to enhance your look."

**Beata Seweryn-Reid**

"A premier smile leads to a premier lifestyle."

**Shonduras (Shaun Todd McBride)**

"Leaders Smile!"

**Frank Sinclair**

"Sometimes life has a tendency to wipe away a smile; God has a tendency to keep you smiling."

**Lisa Sinnott**

"Smiles are the universal expression of positive connection."

**Sean Smiley**

"The fact that I can plant a seed and it becomes a flower, share a bit of knowledge and it becomes another's smile." – Leo Buscaglia

**Jordan Smith**

"Smile with confidence and attract abundance."

**Tanner Smith**

"Smile when you speak and you will speak with love."

**Glenn Stromberg**

"It is a Simple, Mind touching, Interactive, Long Lasting Effect which wins hearts… Yes… It's your "sweet smile," so keep smiling, always!"

**Chris Sullivan**

"Smile so big and so much that it makes people say 'Wow!'"

**Brian Swanson**

"The One Smile you give, can be the smile that makes all the difference."

**Lance Tanaka**

"The secret to happiness is to keep smiling."

**MIke Tenesco**

"Take on every challenge with a smile and you have already increased your chances of success."

**Craig Tomanini**

"A kind heart is a fountain of gladness, making everything in its vicinity freshen into smiles."
–Washington Irving

**Belen Underwood**

"Look back, and smile on perils past."
~Walter Scott

**Gerald Underwood**

"A kind heart is a fountain of gladness, making everything in its vicinity freshen into smiles."
–Washington Irving

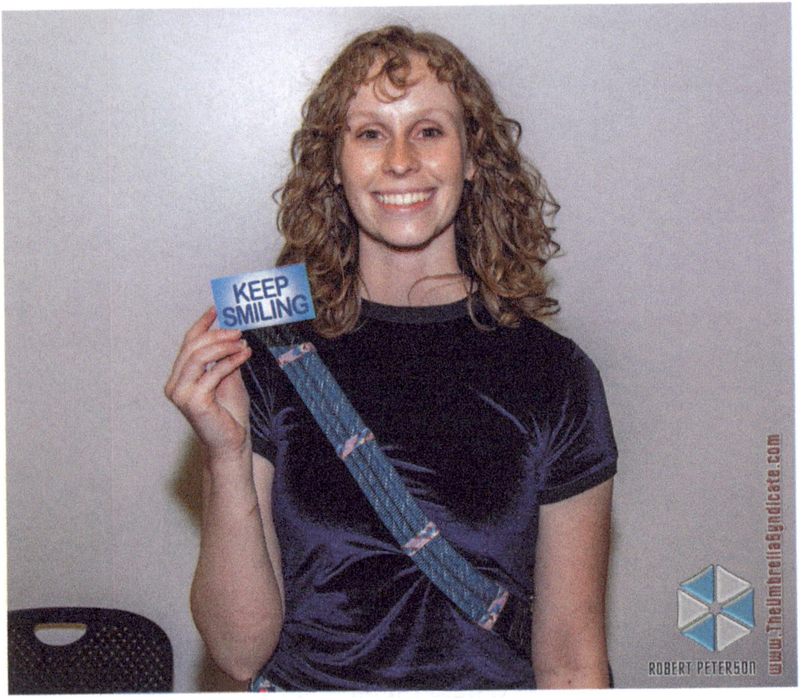


**Jenna VandeBrake-Page**

"Look back, and smile on perils past."
~Walter Scott

**Tom Varano**

"The world always looks brighter from behind a smile." — Unknown

**Pete Vargas**

"A warm smile is the universal language of kindness." – William Arthur Ward

**JJ Villar**

"I love those who can smile in trouble."- Leonardo da Vinci

**Raynei Villareal**

¨Smile at strangers and you just might change a life.¨- Steve Maraboli

**Betsy Waters**

"Nothing you wear is more important than your smile." – Connie Stevens

**Eddie Wilson**

"But God can only smile because only God can know what is coming next." – Desmond Tutu

**Todd Westra**

"The magic of a smile transforms the world."

**Dave Phillipson**

Get your copy of
***The Art of Photobombing***
available special thanks to
Dave Phillipson

**Robert C. Peterson, Mindset Coach; Speaker; Author; Podcaster**

"A smile covers a multitude of mistakes."
– Robert C. Peterson

# FACE ANY CHALLENGE WITH A SMILE

## BY ROBERT C. PETERSON

I have learned the power of a smile. In any situation, a smile can break the ice, portray confidence and cover a multitude of mistakes. A smile changes the attitude of the person smiling and has the power to impact those around them. A smile works when you don't speak the other person's language. A smile is like a social distanced hug.

When I was in eighth grade, we lived in a small town. Middle school was by far my worst school years. I was small, geeky, and felt out of place. I was constantly picked on and poked at. No one was necessarily violent, but just mean. I felt powerless and small.

I had no friends in school and our house was two miles from the nearest neighbor, so my only friend was my little sister and she was still in elementary school.

To be honest, I hated my life. I assume hormones were kicking in. I was angry at the world with no idea how to deal with it. I had an outburst at home once that was so out of control, my mom called our church pastor and told him she thought I was possessed. He didn't have any idea either.

Then there was a chance to change my story. My Father was laid off from his job and the opportunities were in the big city two hours away. He started a new job, we sold our house, and we moved to a new town. It was starting over as a family. We sold what was my parents' dream home and moved into a mobile home. Dad earned half of his previous union salary, so mom went back to work. I started in a new school, and it was my chance to change my story.

I began to smile everyday. I changed my name from my nickname, Bobby, to my given name, Robert. I changed how I carried myself knowing I would be confident being the new me!

In ninth grade, I played on the football team. I had the lead role in the school play. I had perfect attendance. I did great in all of my classes and had other kids asking me for my help. Just like that, I was a different person. I smiled throughout the year, and it was contagious.

I was the same person, yet I was no longer a victim, nor the subject of bullying. In fact, I was approachable, likable and respected. Others wanted to be around me. I finally had friends.

Making this change made high school a much better experience. I became heavily involved in Scouts. My first job was on staff at our local summer camp. That experience kept me motivated enough to earn my rank of Eagle Scout.

High school was a positive experience for the most part. School was fairly easy for me, although I was content to just get by. I was more focused on life outside of school; such as fixing cars, hanging out with friends and trying to attract girls. A group of us had enlisted in the Marines at the end of our junior year, so we knew where we were headed. I had signed a nice contract to be an aircraft mechanic with some bonus money and an early promotion. Thanks to my driving record, a couple of speeding tickets and one silly ticket for illegal lane usage I lost my drivers license. It was only suspended for 45 days because even the motor vehicle hearings officer thought the ticket was silly. The bad news is that the suspension of my drivers license voided my Marine Corps contract. I was still going, but they didn't have to give me the pay or job I had agreed to.

This greatly concerned my dad, who already was struggling with my choosing the Marines. My parents had always assumed I would join the Air Force; with my love of airplanes and the space program. The Marine Corps idea had come out of left field. My friends had invited me to go with them and I decided if I am going to be in combat that I wanted to be trained by the best and be with my friends. Before we shipped out to boot camp, dad asked me, "what if they make you a cook?" I replied that then I will be the best cook that I can be. I was determined to do the best at whatever job I was given.

The first three months of Marine Corps life is basic training and everyone is the same. Most guys know there M.O.S., (Military Occupational Speciality). This is a number that corresponds to a job title. The most common in the Marines is 0311, or Basic Infantry. Near the end of boot camp, we are all sorted into groups based on their MOS. Infantry, engineers, truck drivers, artillery, etc.. Then there is the small group of us who didn't know our MOS. They pull us aside to check a list.

The Drill Instructor looks at the list, and yells out, "Peterson: 4131" Then he stops, turns to the other Drill Instructor and says "4131, what the heck is that?" They actually had to pull out a manual to check. "4131, Marine Corps exchange and Club System." They laugh, like a serious laugh, "what on earth is that?" I had to go back to my unit, to my friends, who are all infantry, artillery, engineers, and tell them that I get to work for the Marine Corps exchange, the only thing I could do was smile in disbelief.

It turns out I was one of the first Marines chosen for a new MOS. A Marine Corps Exchange is like a 7-11 store on the base. I only spent two years working as a Marine exchange Supervisor because I was selected for deployment. I earned two meritorious promotions and made Sergeant E-5 in 30 months. At the time most people didn't earn Sergeant until their 5th or 6th year in service. I made a commitment to do my best at whatever job I was given and to do it with a smile.

After leaving the Marine Corps and returning to Colorado I spent a period of life being lost. I would meet my lovely wife, Noelle, and try a bunch of different jobs. I didn't have a purpose, nothing that I was committed to beyond just getting a paycheck. That just isn't enough to be fulfilled. I needed more.

Noelle and I got involved at her family's church. We went all in, volunteering with the children's ministry to supervise games. I drove the van to pick up folks who couldn't drive to church. I was invited into a discipleship program with the Senior Pastor. We met weekly for a year. I really grew that year. I made the decision to go into ministry and we made the decision to become foreign missionaries. I had to go back to school, but this time, in my mind, it was to be a missionary. I completed 96 credits in two calendar years. I attribute my success to discovering a purpose and the ability to smile about who I was intentionally growing to be.

Later, we spent a year living in Costa Rica learning Spanish. If you have ever learned a second language, you know that you have to smile a lot while laughing at yourself. There is frustration and people who don't understand a thing you say and sometimes all you can do is smile. It takes a great deal of confidence to learn another language and put yourself out in the world to be corrected, ridiculed, and even harassed for saying words wrong. If you aren't willing to say them wrong, then you probably aren't willing to learn.

Next, we moved to Bogotá, Colombia where we coached Colombian Pastors on how to grow their churches. You smile a lot when people don't understand what you are trying to say. You smile as you watch your children grow. Our family spent nine years in Colombia and it will always be home in our hearts. We were blessed to return to Colorado and was hired in a new position to be the Pastor of Outreach for our home church. This created great opportunities for me to travel the world and work with ministries around the globe. Working in this capacity helped me learn the power of a smile across cultures, languages, population and countries.

The biggest lessons I draw from my life is being intentional about what you want to accomplish and who you want to be in the world. Choosing to move towards your future self with a smile on your face is life changing.

• • • • • •

I have always had a heart for people. I have served people as a scout, scout leader, Marine, missionary, pastor and now as a coach. I want to help people grow and live extraordinary lives propelled by their own business dream.

• • • • • •

I really enjoy helping people expand their dreams. It starts with the stories they tell themselves. Together we rewrite their story, allowing them to take full responsibility for their life. They begin to believe in themselves and expand what they believe is possible, and that is worth smiling about. Their future story begins to highlight a journey of lifetime learning, stretching their comfort zone and taking massive action to increase their impact in the world.

# ABOUT ROBERT C. PETERSON

Robert is a husband, father, grandfather, coach, chaplain, author, friend and podcast host. He spent 20 years in ministry guiding others in their leadership while learning techniques to grow himself and them. He and his wife raised their children in Latin America while supporting other missionaries, business owners, and pastors. He is the co-founder of Add Value 2 Life Coaching and co-host of the growing podcast Add Value 2 Entrepreneurs. Robert studied and practiced how to help others in their personal struggles and relationships. He spent those 20 years helping people in their personal lives and now loves helping entrepreneurs change their thinking to take their life and business to another level.

**Books that changed your life:**
The Bible
Think and Grow Rich by Napoleon Hill
Science of Getting Rich by Wallace D. Wattles
As a Man Thinketh by James Allen

**Movies that inspire you:**
The Greatest Showman, Hook

**Songs that inspires you:**
Here Now by Hillsong United
From Now On by Hugh Jackman in The Greatest Showman
I Can Only Imagine by Mercy Me

**Your Hero:**
My dad - who worked hard and saved harder - my lifelong friend

**Quote you live by:**
"I can do all things through Christ who strengthens me." Philippians 4:13

# Hire Robert as a Speaker

Robert is an international speaker who has travelled and taught in more than a dozen countries.

He shares powerful stories of transformation and his dynamic style will engage your audience and leave them ready to take action in their own lives.

Email Admin@AddValue2Life.com for more information.

# Ready to Hear More?

Entrepreneurs get stuck in their head, challenged by their thoughts, the voice in their head and their beliefs. We help them get out of their own way.

We chat with successful entrepreneurs who share their journey and the lessons learned along the way.

The show is fun and encouraging while maintaining a level of professional excellence. We talk business but we also ask about a favorite date night or how they spend their free time.

Add Value 2 Entrepreneurs is edu-taining, leaving the audience with actionable advice they can apply to their own work and life.

Our host Robert Peterson is a thinking coach focused on mindset, beliefs and manifestation. Our co-host Noelle Peterson is the heartbeat behind our company, coaching in leadership and process development.

AddValue2Entrepreneurs.com

**Ken 'Dr. Smiley' Rochon, Jr., PhD**

"A smile amplifies goodness."
– Ken Rochon

# ABOUT KEN 'DR. SMILEY' ROCHON, JR., PhD

Ken Rochon, Jr. is an internationally recognized dynamic speaker, author, social media expert and connector. He is a renaissance spiritual leader, who loves the arts, sciences and people.

After losing his mom to Alzheimer's disease in 2008, he searched for the ultimate meaning and purpose for his life. He prayed for a sign that would allow him to dedicate his life to service and utilize his skill sets to amplify leaders making a positive impact in the world.

Ken's ability to capture and captivate the human spirit at live events, on the radio, through speaking, photography and writing are highly recognized as evidenced in the multiple hundreds of reviews and recommendations. His love for his mom cause him to take more actions, which resulted in the sign he prayed for. His evidence was the avalanche multiple hundreds of 5-Star reviews and recommendations. Ken is creating a dynamic positive impact and building a legacy for himself and other leaders. He is Internationally recognized as an influencer that uses his gifts and creates platforms and systems to amplify the messages of leaders that desire to change the world.

"Ken Rochon is a master at creating social proof. He and The Umbrella Syndicate team are fantastic with guests and really know how to connect everyone in the room. He consistently produces fantastic work and we are always so happy to have him speak and photograph at our You Will Change The World summits and masterminds" Peter Anthony Wynn, Founder of 'You Will Change The World'

The Umbrella Syndicate (TUS) was created, by Ken, with six elements represented by each segment of the umbrella that strategically and synergistically move the vision of a leader beyond their own minds eye. He studied strategies of leveraging like-minded and like hearted audiences to create these epic social proof campaigns for the leaders he chose to serve. Ken has created a formula that captures and catapults the message that wakes the world up with a positive frequency that inspires people to learn more.

"Ken and the Umbrella Team are probably the most proactive, positive and professional media I have ever seen. If you want viral videos and photography, creative coverage and incredible insights into your event, brand or persona, they are the top of the food chain." Dave Crane

Ken is lifetime entrepreneur, starting in his teen years, founding and delivering excellence with the award winning company Absolute Entertainment. He continues as a visionary and leader with companies and movements such as; The Perfect Networker, Live Loco Love Studio, The Perfect Publishing Ken has authored 17 books on diverse topics; children, linguistics, marketing, networking, and travel. He has published over 50 solo and compilation books. His current book 'Keep Smiling Shift Happens!' has caused a movement of celebrities and leaders t to join in helping remind the world positivity, with just a simple smile, attracts positive power.

"At the end of the day public relations, marketing are about communicating a story. The "HOW" is identical: Get customers. Move product. Drive revenue. Our WHY is what positions us to change the world." I love to travel because I learn so much about myself and others. I recently accomplished becoming a Centurion Traveler by experiencing over 100 countries. My favorite place to travel is back home. My son Kenny is the light of his life and a moment by moment inspiration of my purpose in life." Ken Rochon, Jr.

https://youtu.be/7IDcwQB0Fj4

# ABOUT ANDREA ADAMS-MILLER

Andrea Adams-Miller, CEO, The RED Carpet Connection, & Executive Director, the Keep Smiling Movement, Inc, is the machine behind your business that moves dreams into action resulting in a reality never dreamt possible.

With a whirlwind of energy, a passion for success, and a deep desire for long-lasting professional relationships, she makes the right connections, devises the best solutions, and implements the smartest marketing tactics to increase your Authority, Credibility, and Income in more ways than one!

Trust in Andrea to spotlight your business and find you the sponsors you deserve, and enlist Ken and Andrea to cover your RED Carpet conferences and grace your radio, television, and magazines to share how your event and the power of smiles, the universal expression of love, impact the world's Happiness Index.

Call Andrea 419-722-6931, AndreaAdamsMiller@
TheREDCarpetConnection.com

KEEP SMILING
IMPACT HAPPENS!
INFLUENCER COLOR EDITION
KEN ROCHON, JR.
KEEP SMILING
SHIFT HAPPENS!
KEN ROCHON, JR.

Want to be in our next edition?
KEEP SMILING
KEEP SMILING
KEEP SMILING
KEEP SMILING
KEEP SMILING
KEEP SMILING
• AUTHORS • SPEAKERS •
• LEADERS • ACTORS • ARTISTS •
• MODELS • MUSICIANS • DENTISTS •
• ORTHODONTIST •
VISIT OUR STUDIO
IN BALTIMORE OR DC AREA
ken@BIGeventsUSA.com | 202•701•0911
7513 Connelley Dr, Ste K, Hanover, MD 21076
LIVE•LOCO•LOVE
STUDIO

**Making smiles on the outside creates smiles in the inside**

## Color

- **Name on Front Cover**
- Customized Cover
- 4-6 page chapter about how Smiles have changed your life / How you have changed someone's life by giving them a smile
- 1-2 page bio about you and your profession with contact info
- **50 customized photos of your patients holding 'Keep Smiling' cards included in the book.**

**100 Quantity – $5000**
**Additional 100 is only $1995**
**Additional 400 is only $3495**

Order today!

(202) 701-0911 • info@theumbrellasyndicate.com

# THE ART OF SERIES

BY KEN ROCHON, JR.

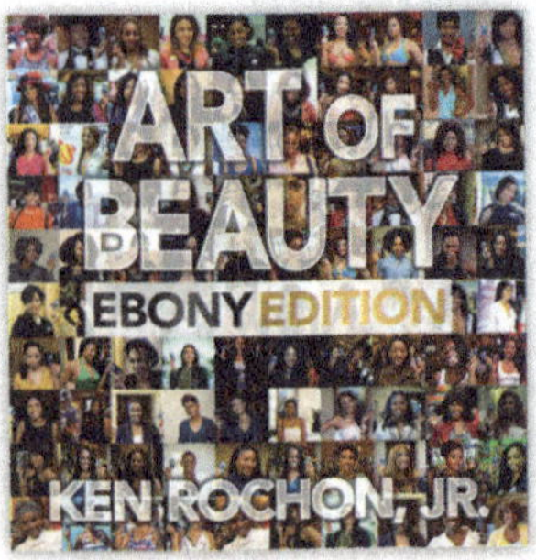

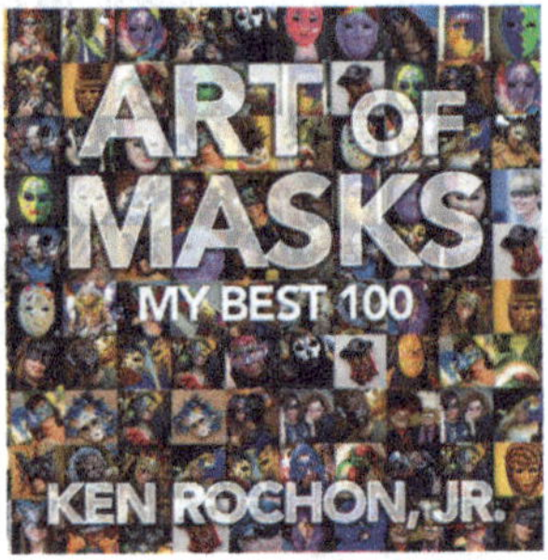


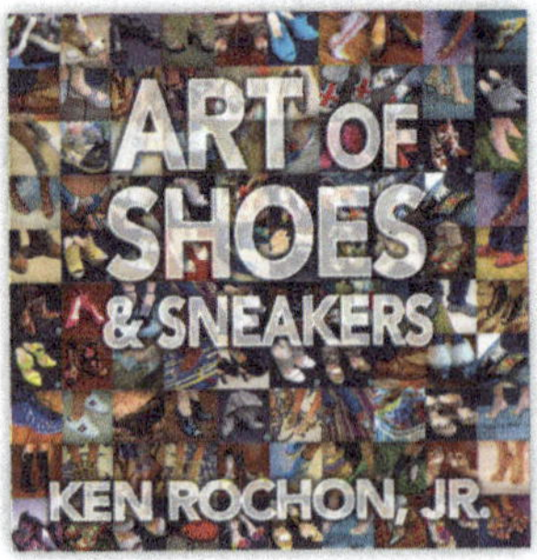


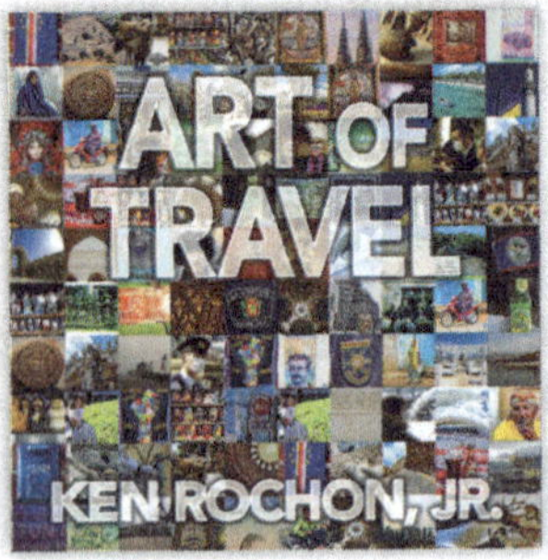


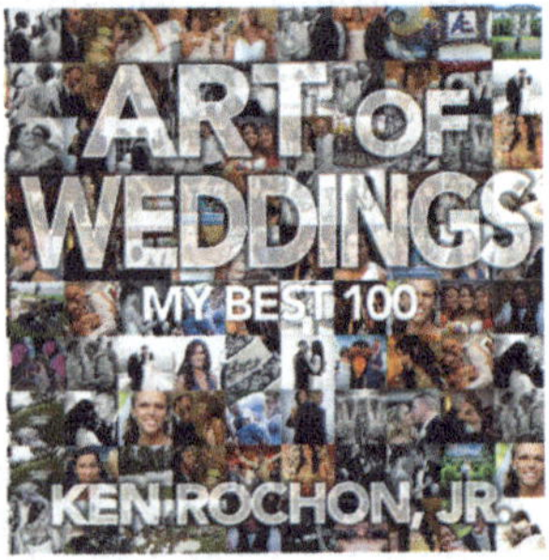

Made in United States
Orlando, FL
04 November 2026

90194944R00089